CONTENTS

THE INTRODUCTION OF A MENTAL HEALTH COMPONENT INTO PRIMARY HEALTH CARE

WORLD HEALTH ORGANIZATION
GENEVA
1990

WHO Library Cataloguing in Publication Data

The introduction of a mental health component into
    primary health care.

    1.Community mental health services   2.Primary health
    care – organization & administration

    ISBN 92 4 156136 X   (NLM Classification: WM 30)

TYPESET IN INDIA
PRINTED IN ENGLAND
89/8095—Macmillans/Clays—4000

PREFACE

The World Health Organization has long stressed the need for mental health care to be decentralized and integrated into primary health care, with the necessary tasks carried out as far as possible by general health workers rather than by specialists in mental health. During the 1970s, a WHO Collaborative Study on Strategies for Extending Mental Health Care, in seven developing countries, set the pattern for this process. Following a critical review of this and other recent work, it was decided that it would be useful to set out the practical steps necessary to introduce a mental health component into primary health care. To achieve this, WHO brought together a number of experts at the WHO Collaborating Centre for Research and Training in Mental Health in Groningen, the Netherlands, in December 1985.

The first draft produced at that meeting was circulated widely, and many people made suggestions for improvement; special mention must be made of the work carried out by Dr G. A. German.

During the 1980s, WHO has worked with Member States in their efforts to introduce mental health care into national health programmes. This book sets out a framework within which this can be done.

*   *   *

WHO wishes to thank the following people who contributed to this publication:

Dr E. D'A. Busnello (Brazil), Dr G. A. German (Australia), Dr R. Giel (Netherlands), Dr T. Harding (Switzerland), Dr J. Hauli (United Republic of Tanzania), Dr L. Ladrido-Ignacio (Philippines), Dr R. S. Murthy (India), Dr J. Orley (WHO, Geneva), Dr H. Sell (WHO Regional Office for South-East Asia, Delhi), Dr G. H. M. M. ten Horn (Netherlands), Dr N. Wig (WHO Regional Office for the Eastern Mediterranean, Alexandria) and Dr F. Workneh (Ethiopia).

Chapter 1

MENTAL HEALTH ISSUES IN PRIMARY HEALTH CARE

The need for more appropriate and flexible methods of health delivery

Existing systems for the delivery of health care, including mental health care, have largely failed to meet the needs of most of the world's population. Many of the systems are centralized, hospital-based, and disease-oriented, with care delivered by medical personnel in a one-to-one doctor/patient relationship. Such care is often inconsistent with the principle of social equity, particularly in developing countries.

WHO's Member States have agreed that the key to achieving their goal of health for all by the year 2000 is primary health care. This is care based on the needs of populations, rather than on the needs of health structures and centralized specialist facilities; it is decentralized, requires the active participation of the community and family, and is undertaken by nonspecialized general health workers collaborating with personnel in other governmental and nongovernmental sectors. These general health workers should be trained in the use of simple but effective techniques that are widely applicable, such as mobilizing community action, stimulating self-help groups, and providing health education, with particular emphasis on health promotion and disease prevention. The health sector should be structured to support these decentralized activities. The key components are thus decentralization, delegation of certain medical tasks to general health care workers and to the people themselves, and a permeation of health knowledge and techniques into other sectors, utilizing non-health personnel to promote health.

The emphasis on the people themselves taking responsibility for their health is an important aspect of the development of people and communities. Too often an effective primary health care system is seen as a more efficient, humane and effective "delivery" system; it delivers a commodity, namely health, which should in fact be within the ability of people to obtain for themselves. Health should, as far as possible, never be "given to" or "provided for" people. On the contrary, people should be helped to be constantly and actively involved in securing and promoting their own health.

The change in policy towards health for all is sometimes seen as an attack on the high standards of care provided in centres of excellence. It may at times be resisted by some medical personnel who see decentralization of health care as a threat to their status. In fact, within a primary health care system, specialist health personnel will have to assume vital leadership roles which can only enhance their status. However, the shift towards increased teamwork—which may be less easy than the conventional work patterns where the worker is located only within a consulting room or clinic—will require the development of educational, persuasive, interpersonal, and teamwork skills in health personnel and hence a new approach to training.[1] It is important that senior medical personnel should see that the very clear role required of them in effecting these changes enhances rather than lowers their status.

Mental health care: a neglected component

No health service or system is complete without attention to the mental health needs of populations; it cannot be effective without incorporating concern for people's mental welfare. Nevertheless, apart from providing specialized facilities for the treatment of mental disease, most existing health systems ignore the mental aspect of human life. They usually fail to take account of the impact of emotion and behaviour on health. Existing training patterns for most health workers, particularly physicians, concentrate on specific diseases, neglecting the concept of people as whole organisms who, in turn, are an intimate part of a much wider social environment. The human body cannot be treated as a collection of organs which may sometimes need repair, nor can an individual be treated in isolation from society. As a result, while techniques for the management of disease advance, more and more patients complain about an excessive preoccupation with technology at the expense of human considerations; they feel alienated from health care providers and institutions, and they often do not comply with recommended public health measures. Many people throughout the world lack a sense of physical, psychological and social well-being; they may perceive shortcomings in their surroundings, in their way of life, or in the availability of health care. Adequate health care, therefore, must produce more than freedom from disease: it must also promote an individual and community sense of well-being.

---

[1] WHO Technical Report Series, No. 746, 1987 (*Community-based education of health personnel*: report of a WHO Study Group).

The Constitution of the World Health Organization, accepted by all WHO's Member States, defines health as a state of complete physical, mental and social well-being, with no indication that any one of these should have precedence over another. To achieve such a state of well-being, it is vital that health provision be based on a holistic approach to the individual and to the community. Attention to mental and social well-being has too often been neglected in the training of health workers and the delivery of health care.

Primary health care, with its greater emphasis on activities undertaken by workers at community level, has challenged the assumption that mental health problems are unimportant. Indeed, such problems account for a significant part of the work at community level. For instance, in curative services it has often been considered that one function of peripheral workers is to screen patients presenting for health care. They are sometimes expected to turn away those with psychological and social problems and select from among the physically ill whom to treat and whom to refer. To gain acceptance within a community and to act as a health leader, however, a health worker has to be sensitive to psychological and social problems, and be able to cope with them rather than dismiss them as irrelevant. It is not just for the sake of good public relations that a health worker should deal with them; they are legitimate health problems as much as are physical problems and deserve attention in their own right. Moreover, the psychological state of an individual influences his or her physical state and thus deserves attention if proper treatment is to be given or preventive programmes implemented.

A health worker who works in the community is more likely to see a patient in the natural setting of home or workplace. Because of this, the patient is frequently seen with other people, and the psychological and social dimensions of his or her life become more obvious. In these circumstances, it is particularly inappropriate for the health worker to treat the patient as an isolated being, or his or her disease as the condition of a single organ.

The introduction of a mental health component into primary health care is essential. Such a component is more than a matter of treating mental disease: it has a bearing on all aspects of health care at both individual and community levels. A state of psychological and social well-being does not automatically result from a state of physical well-being. Of course, physical disease of itself leads to distress, but it is just as appropriate for health workers to respond directly to psychological and social needs as to physical symptoms. Indeed, a failure to take account of a patient's psychological needs frequently leads to a failure of treatment directed at a particular physical condition.

**ATTENTION TO MENTAL HEALTH IS ESSENTIAL
IF PRIMARY HEALTH CARE IS TO BE USEFUL**

Patients often see a health worker because of psychological and emotional distress rather than because of an obvious physical illness. Such patients frequently have physical complaints and it is vital that the health worker is able to recognize that these symptoms may reflect psychological problems. Physical complaints are often a way of expressing psychosocial distress, and failure to recognize this can lead to wastage of health resources. Furthermore, human behaviour is an important factor in generating and maintaining disease, and effective prevention and treatment must therefore concentrate on changing behaviour. This requires the skilful application of psychological principles by all health workers.

In conclusion, it should surprise no one that the recommendations of the Alma-Ata Conference emphasized that the promotion of good mental health should be a component of primary health care. This does not mean only the diagnosis and treatment of mental disorders (psychiatry). Good mental health care is properly part of all those activities subsumed under the treatment of common diseases, and as such is an essential element of adequate primary health care. Even this, however, is not the most important aspect of promoting mental health: it is still more important that in all activities for the promotion of health there is a concern for psychological well-being and the quality of mental life. Mental health should receive special attention in every aspect of health activity, and should be included as an important element of primary health care.

Chapter 2

THE SCOPE OF MENTAL HEALTH IN PRIMARY HEALTH CARE

The mental health component of health care comprises two quite distinct areas which, unfortunately, are often confused.

The first emphasizes the practical relevance of psychosocial and behavioural science skills in general health care. These skills are of vital importance in:

— improving the functioning of general health services;

— supporting overall socioeconomic development;

— enhancing the quality of life;

— promoting mental and emotional health.

These have seldom formed part of the tasks actually assigned to health care workers, and this needs to change.

The second area concerns the control of mental and neurological diseases. This area is better understood by health professionals in general, but at the same time has often been regarded as too highly specialized to be part of the responsibility of general health workers. Research suggests, however, that general health personnel are capable of managing many mental and neurological disorders. Two aspects require consideration:

— prevention of mental and neurological disorders;

— diagnosis and treatment (including rehabilitation) of people with mental or neurological disorders.

It might be thought that the extensive scope of mental health activities would add greatly to the tasks of the general health worker at the expense of the efficient delivery of other aspects of health care, such as maternal and child health care, control of infectious diseases, and the promotion of adequate nutrition. However, it is not a matter of *adding* a mental health component: there is overwhelming evidence that mental health problems are already present among general health problems, but that they are either unnoticed or ignored. Valuable resources are often wasted through failure to recognize these problems, which are therefore dealt with inadequately. This leads to patient dissatisfaction, chronicity, and further wastage of resources.

RESPONSIBILITY FOR MENTAL HEALTH IS NOT AN EXTRA LOAD FOR PRIMARY HEALTH CARE SERVICES; ON THE CONTRARY, IT INCREASES THEIR EFFECTIVENESS

By making health workers sensitive to the presence of mental health problems, and by equipping them with the skills to deal with those problems, much wastage of effort in general health work can be avoided and health care can be made more effective. It might be noted that the discovery of the role of microorganisms in disease, far from placing an additional burden on health workers, enabled time-wasting and inappropriate approaches to be abandoned and made the management of infectious disease much more efficient. Neglect of the psychological and social components of health, and the behavioural aspects of illness, has been—and remains—a fundamental error of existing health systems.

Improving the functioning of general health services

The effectiveness of health care workers has been shown to be greatly increased by improving their skills in interviewing and counselling. For instance, it has been shown that, if physicians do not write notes while listening to a patient, their diagnostic efficiency is substantially increased. There is also clear evidence that the introduction of counselling into general medical practice reduces the number of drugs prescribed and the investigations performed. Training primary health workers in interpersonal skills greatly improves their ability to mobilize self-care and mutual support groups within the community. It also helps them to persuade voluntary groups to contribute to health objectives, particularly those relating to the disabled, disadvantaged and vulnerable.

Emotional signs of physical risk

Recent research has shown that emotional and psychological distress may be an early manifestation of physical disease processes, or may itself cause such disease processes. For example, the stress of bereavement and the depression that may follow have been associated with measurable reductions in the efficiency of immune mechanisms, and with increased vulnerability to infectious disease, neoplasia, and acute cardiac failure. Depressive illness has been shown to be a common early manifestation of the development of cancer, presenting well before more specific physical symptoms in many cases. It has also been shown to precede acute myocardial infarction at a much more than chance level of frequency. Thus emotional and psychological changes in client populations cannot be ignored in any consideration of general health status, nor can they be ignored in the analysis of risk factors in individual cases.

Behaviour can cause illness

Many chronic and disabling disorders follow from certain forms of behaviour. For instance, use of drugs, such as nicotine, alcohol or tranquillizers, has been identified as playing a major part in the development of serious health problems such as lung cancer and gastrointestinal and liver disease, as well as in the development of common problems, such as hypertension, which may lead to more serious disease. Human behaviour also plays a major role in the transmission of infectious and parasitic diseases, and in failure to achieve adequate maternal and child health, effective family planning, and good nutrition. It is sometimes mistakenly thought that such behaviour is a result of ignorance. There are, however, features of an individual's personal, emotional, and social life that commonly lead to the persistence of unhealthy behavioural patterns, even in well-informed populations. The identification and management of such socially and emotionally determined aspects of behaviour therefore become an essential part of the delivery of good health care.

Medical technology is not enough to produce good health

In general it can be said that the current practice of medicine in many countries relies too heavily on technology. Psychosocial skills that could make the health worker more efficient, and more satisfied with his or her work, are seldom taught. Many populations are becoming more and more dissatisfied with the care they receive, in spite of increased expenditure on the health services. Mental health and behavioural science disciplines can provide some of the knowledge and skills necessary to reverse this process, and it is therefore important to ensure that these are incorporated in the training and practice of all general health staff.

Psychological and emotional states play an important role in determining whether or not medical intervention is beneficial. Patients may fail to comply with drug prescriptions for a variety of psychological reasons. Treatment regimes may be rendered useless because of negative or resentful patient attitudes which may, for instance, relate to the way in which a particular treatment programme is perceived (e.g. tablets might be thought less effective than injections).

The relationship between the patient and the health worker is also important and health workers who are seen as unsympathetic or antagonistic are less likely to be effective in the delivery of treatment, and their advice may be deliberately ignored. Similarly, some hospitals and clinics may be viewed negatively. Some of these attitudes may prevail in entire populations; at other times the negative attitude of an individual patient must be recognized and dealt with before medical intervention is likely to be successful or acceptable.

Contributions to socioeconomic development

Although social development often leads to psychosocial problems, some of the adverse consequences of development projects may be avoided by taking account of people's psychosocial needs. Comprehensive mental health programmes should collaborate with those responsible for planning and economic development, and provide insights that may make social change more compatible with people's expectations and psychological needs.

Conversely, socioeconomic development is hindered by emotional and psychological disability and distress. This impairment may be made worse by problems such as drug and alcohol abuse, rising statistics of road traffic accidents, the breakdown of family and traditional systems, and public and community violence. Moreover, one of the most important causes of absenteeism in industry is the occurrence of vague feelings of emotional and psychological ill-health and lack of well-being. These and other psychosocial problems, the management of which has hardly been tackled, place great burdens on communities everywhere, particularly in the developing world where resources to meet and deal with them are few. Equipping general health personnel and others involved in social development with appropriate mental and psychosocial skills would help to make health interventions more effective and social development less distressing. Psychosocial sensitivity is not a matter of expensive technology but of promoting human skills in all personnel with a role in socioeconomic development.

Enhancing the quality of life

The achievement of an enhanced quality of life needs more than just the prevention and treatment of disease; there must also be a concern to promote physical, psychological and social well-being. Primary health care workers trained in mental health and behavioural skills can play an important role in all these areas, particularly when their work involves making regular home visits.

Many members of the population may be free from identifiable disease, but this is not necessarily synonymous with their achieving optimum physical, mental and social well-being. Techniques developed in recent years, which primary health care workers might use to promote such well-being, include education in methods of combating stress (e.g. relaxation and meditation techniques), use of leisure time (e.g. recreational activities, sport, regular exercise), and methods of maintaining social support systems (involvement in community projects and development activities).

SIMPLE SKILLS CAN IMPROVE LIFE

Appropriately trained primary health care workers can have a substantial impact on the quality of life through their involvement in slum improvement or rural development projects. In many instances, the health promotion and disease management components of primary health care services become acceptable to communities only when primary health care workers take an active part in community development.

Primary health care services can also help in the area of child development, particularly for children from socially disadvantaged backgrounds. If such children can be identified, their prospects can be much improved through early stimulation programmes carried out, for instance, by volunteer groups. Primary health workers should be able to identify families with obvious problems, in which the children are at special risk of understimulation, neglect, injury or malnutrition. Identification of "risk families" is of great importance in allowing health workers to deal with their special needs, and to plan interventions at community as well as family level.

The promotion of mental health

Promotion of mental health requires a sensitive awareness in health workers of the importance of mental and emotional well-being in the scale of values of the people they serve. Individuals may not express their need for well-being in terms of mental health, in that the word "mental" may be stigmatized and misunderstood, but they do seek relief from unhappiness, distress, and impaired psychosocial functioning. On a day-to-day basis people are generally more concerned with their enjoyment of life, their morale, and their interactions with other people than they are with their physical health.

PEOPLE NEED MORE THAN PHYSICAL CARE

In promoting mental health it is perhaps particularly important that the health worker be deeply involved with community aspirations and goals. Individuals, families, and communities need to define what they require to improve their enjoyment of life and certainly need to participate in the discussion of such matters. Social and cultural values play an important part in the evolution of good mental health in any society.

The mental health care of women is an area in which improvement is especially necessary. Women in many societies are not able, at present, to achieve full social or educational development because of cultural attitudes towards their role in society. In many instances, the education of girls is given much less attention than that of boys; women may also be expected to do menial jobs and be paid less for their work. As a result their mental and emotional development suffers. These women cannot be said to be mentally ill in the accepted sense of the term, but their problems relate to a failure to achieve and enjoy optimum mental health. Their situation well illustrates the difference between concerns about mental illness on the one hand and concerns about promoting good mental health on the other.

Mental health workers, acting in collaboration with communities, may be able to influence attitudes and promote changes that will benefit women in the community. For example, there could be encouragement for girls to attend school and for women to organize various self-help activities that would promote their greater well-being, such as collective day-care for children.

Another area in which positive mental health promotion is important is that of drug and alcohol abuse. Here the concern is not with the more serious manifestations of abuse, which include addictions and other biomedical problems, but rather with the mismanagement of alcohol and drugs to the detriment of mental health and family happiness. Even patterns of alcohol use that are accepted by many cultures as normal and even socially desirable may be hindering full development of mental health through ignorance of the effects of alcohol. The evidence is overwhelming that most people are physically and mentally healthier in a drug-free environment, and promotion of such values may be an important part of the work of a primary health worker. Other attitudes worthy of development are those relating to good eating habits, regular exercise, and physical fitness.

The primary health worker must be concerned to educate the community about such matters and, in a more subtle way, to assist in the development of positive attitudes that contribute to the well-being of disadvantaged groups and lead to better management of social and environmental activities.

Prevention of mental and neurological disorders

The prevention of a significant proportion of mental, neurological and psychosocial disorders is now possible. It has been estimated that at least half of all such disorders in developing countries can be prevented by methods that are simple and effective and that cost little. Much of the preventive work should be done by the general health services and through the intervention of other agencies, such as community development, agricultural extension and education services. The specialized mental health profession often has a lesser role in the direct sense, although it may be a most important one in terms of educating colleagues.

The following are examples of preventive measures:

— The provision of iodinated salt or injections of iodinated oil to women of childbearing age in areas of iodine deficiency helps prevent mental retardation in their children.

— Emotional and intellectual stimulation of children, together with the identification and correction of sensory defects (e.g. poor sight, impaired hearing), can markedly reduce the number of children labelled as mentally retarded and also significantly enhance the development of children generally.

— Crisis intervention (e.g. support to the recently bereaved) and education of parents in child-rearing practices can produce significant health benefits.

The primary prevention of mental ill-health places particular emphasis on the education of families and children; teachers and other influential members of the community have a vital role in this, complementary to that of the primary health care worker. Through their efforts the development of alcohol and drug abuse can be curtailed, and the negative effects of deprivation and under-stimulation on the mental health of children can be reduced.

Detection and treatment of mental disease

The burden of mental illness is a heavy one, both for the patient and for his or her family. However, the treatment that is now available for the mentally ill need not be expensive, nor need it be administered by highly specialized personnel. It has been established that general health workers in community health centres and dispensaries are capable of identifying and managing even severe mental disorders. A variety of such treatments suitable for use within a primary health care system are now available and have been shown to be both inexpensive and effective. Pilot studies in a number of countries have demonstrated that non-specialists can provide an effective foundation for a mental health care programme.

MENTAL ILLNESS DOES NOT ALWAYS NEED
SPECIALIST TREATMENT

This should not be taken to mean that mental health specialists have become redundant; their role in this context should be one of providing supervision and training. Appropriate supervision of nonspecialist health care workers is an essential component of the introduction of mental health care into general health work, without which the effectiveness of primary health care programmes would be in doubt.

Mental disorders requiring intervention by health care workers fall into four groups: severe disorders such as senile dementia and schizophrenia, the more common and milder psychological and emotional disturbances, drug and alcohol abuse and dependence, and psychological problems arising as a consequence of physical disease or injury.

Severe mental disorders account for between 1% and 5% of mental health problems seen at the primary health care level. They include the conditions that many people class as "madness"—the psychoses (schizophrenia, depressive illness), dementias and other organic brain syndromes, and neurological disorders such as epilepsy and the consequences of head injuries. Because of the disruption these illnesses can cause, the fear they induce and the stigma they attract from the community as a whole, they are the source of great distress, not only for the sufferer but also for his or her family. Where knowledge of mental illness is lacking, feelings of helplessness and panic are aroused, even among health workers. The disorders are frequently chronic and patients may live for many years, their presence imposing a considerable burden on other family members who may themselves become increasingly prone to stress-related illness as a consequence. Patients may even be rejected by family and friends and become social outcasts or vagrants. Even where the disorder takes an acute form and will eventually resolve, rejection by the community may still arise from the fear that the problem will recur.

Medical intervention in the past frequently consisted of sending patients as quickly as possible to distant custodial mental hospitals. It is now known, however, that a substantial number—possibly a majority—of serious mental disorders are relatively easy to treat, using methods that can be undertaken by primary health care workers. Even chronic conditions can be effectively controlled with long-term maintenance treatment by primary health personnel working under supervision. Hospitalization for accurate diagnosis and initiation of treatment may occasionally be necessary, but otherwise adequate management can be effected at health centre or village level. Such management—within the community and coordinated by primary health care workers and their supervisors—is highly cost-effective and avoids much disruption to the patients' family life.

SEVERE MENTAL ILLNESS CAN BE MANAGED OUTSIDE HOSPITAL

Less severe types of psychological disturbance and mental illness are more common but often less easily recognized. They include neuroses, acute emotional stress in response to crises such as bereavement, chronic stress arising from long-term social and/or economic difficulties, aberrant behaviour resulting from personality disorders, and developmental problems in children and adolescents. Estimates from both developed and developing countries suggest that this type of complaint accounts for between 20% and 40% of all illness treated in general health care facilities.

Although classed as "less severe", these disorders may well become chronic unless dealt with effectively, and can be the cause of extensive disruption within the family and the community. Possibly their greatest significance lies in the fact that patients frequently present with physical symptoms such as pain, nausea, sexual difficulties, sleep problems, fatigue, lack of appetite and weight loss.

PHYSICAL COMPLAINTS CAN BE CAUSED BY MENTAL ILLNESS

Research has indicated that it is not uncommon for general health personnel to fail to diagnose this type of mental disorder. As a consequence, repeated and expensive investigations may be undertaken in the attempt to find physical causes for the symptoms, numerous ineffective and costly medications may be prescribed and patients may visit many different health facilities in a fruitless search for effective treatment. Scarce health resources are thus frequently wasted, and patients may be needlessly exposed to drugs that do nothing to help them and may actually give rise to dependence and further mental and emotional difficulties.

When problems of this nature are correctly identified, however, relatively simple forms of intervention can be of great value. In the short term, support and counselling can be provided both for patients and for their families; where necessary, appropriate psychoactive medication may be prescribed until physical and mental symptoms subside.

In most countries the proportion of mental—and often physical—illness attributable to the abuse of alcohol and other drugs is sufficiently large to merit special attention. Alcohol abuse is the most widespread such problem in the majority of cases, and one that is likely to become worse in many developing countries as commercial production and sales of alcoholic drinks increase. Alcohol-related health problems have been shown to include depression and obesity, as well as less common but often more serious complaints such as liver and gastrointestinal disease. Accidental injuries are common in alcohol abuse, and psychosocial problems may include family disharmony, stress-related illness in other family members, and suicide (including attempted suicide).

PHYSICAL AND EMOTIONAL COMPLAINTS OFTEN CONCEAL ALCOHOL AND DRUG ABUSE

The commonest types of drug abuse problem will vary from country to country; in some countries they will be associated with drugs that have long been available, while in others they will be linked to drugs that have only recently been introduced on a wide scale. The extent to which any particular drug gives rise to problems of abuse in a particular area depends not only on the toxicity and dependence potential of the drug but also upon its availability, acceptability and method of administration and the distribution of its use in different age, social and ethnic groups. Health workers should be fully aware of the drugs that are used— and abused—within their area[1] and constantly mindful of the potential risks associated with the prescribing of some of the very drugs that are most useful in managing mental disorders.[2] Additional vigilance is essential in areas where illicit drugs are commonly injected and the transmission of serious diseases such as viral hepatitis B and acquired immunodeficiency syndrome (AIDS) is a substantial risk.

Psychological problems resulting from physical illness—particularly chronic illness—may give rise to complications that are more serious than the original disorder. In both developed and developing countries, for example, chronic pain, disability and other serious physical complaints have been found to be significant factors in the incidence of suicide. During and after almost any serious illness, patients are likely to manifest some form of emotional disturbance, which may be so severe as to become disabling. Less dramatic, but more frequent, are the stresses that arise in families and communities caring for the chronically sick.

PHYSICAL ILLNESS CAN CAUSE MENTAL DISORDER

Psychological symptoms of this nature can lead to errors in medical diagnosis. Indeed, prejudice against psychologically disturbed patients may lead to their rejection and to a treatable physical illness being neglected. It is essential that health workers show sensitivity to the psychological complications of illness and treat the patient as a whole; in this way psychosocial distress can be significantly lessened and the efficacy with which the primary complaint is managed greatly improved.

---

[1] See: *Drug dependence and alcohol-related problems. A manual for community health workers with guidelines for trainers.* Geneva, World Health Organization, 1986.
[2] GHODSE, H. & KHAN, I. *Psychoactive drugs: improving prescribing practices.* Geneva, World Health Organization, 1988.

Mental health issues have a vital contribution to make in the social and psychological development of societies and must permeate every aspect of general health work. Just as notions of hygiene and asepsis came to the fore in health-related activities in the late nineteenth century, so now there is an urgent need for psychosocial awareness and sensitivity to receive more prominence in the training and activities of health workers. Existing health education and practice, particularly in developing countries, tends to neglect the broader aspects of mental health. Changes in practice will require changes in attitude by planners and health workers alike, and are essential if health care work is to be effective and resources conserved.

> HEALTH IS IMPOSSIBLE IF EMOTIONAL NEEDS ARE
> NEGLECTED

Chapter 3

THE IMPORTANCE OF A NATIONAL MENTAL HEALTH POLICY

A strong mental health programme is an essential component of any effective health care system. Where a mental health policy and related mental health programme are lacking, high priority must be given to their development as an integral part of the overall national health programme. This may require a positive and concerted act of political will if the stigma that so often attaches to the subject of mental illness is to be overcome. Ideally a governmental, rather than ministerial, statement of national mental health policy should be issued, stressing the need for involvement of other sectors as well as health in its implementation. Only coordinated action by a range of governmental bodies and nongovernmental organizations can produce a comprehensive mental health care programme.

Examples of policy statements

The precise details of any national mental health policy will vary according to the philosophies, ideals and circumstances of the particular country. In general, however, policies that have proved to be valuable include such commitments as the following:

- At all levels, mental health services should be integrated as far as possible with general health services.

- Comprehensive coverage of populations demands that delivery of mental health care be firmly established in the primary health care setting and promoted by those who are not mental health specialists.

- Appropriate training in mental health and psychosocial skills is essential for all health personnel, and also for many working in other sectors, for example education, community development, social welfare, and police forces.

- Steps should be taken to promote healthy attitudes in young people that will prevent aberrant behaviour with adverse consequences for health.

- Management of health problems associated with alcohol and drug abuse should be an integral component of the national mental health policy.

- Individuals suffering from mental disorders should have the same rights to treatment and support as those with physical disorders.

- Individuals suffering from mental disorders should be treated within or as close as possible to their own communities, using local resources.

Coordinating groups for mental health

The development of a national mental health policy will depend in part on political ideals and in part on a variety of technical contributions. In many countries it has proved valuable to establish national coordinating groups, with membership drawn from various sectors such as other ministries and nongovernmental organizations, including religious and voluntary groups involved in individual and community growth and development. Because of the stigma often attached to mental health issues, it has proved important that people appointed to a coordinating group be of senior ministerial rank or in a position otherwise to exercise influence and authority. Coordinating groups can be charged with sampling a wide range of opinion from professionals, consultants, health administrators and planners, experts in sectors such as social services, education and law, and university research bodies. They can also ensure that a mental health programme is responsive to what people feel their needs to be. On occasion, co-ordinating groups have submitted ideas to a national conference before making final recommendations on a mental health policy.

Policies should lead to programmes

The next step, the development of a national mental health programme, might also usefully involve a coordinating group, which would again enable many sectors, both governmental and nongovernmental, to participate in the process. Although such groups can advise the ministry of health, their principal function should be to ensure that each sector has a clear understanding of what its own activities should be and that such activities are coordinated.

Programme development requires that data be obtained on the prevalence of psychosocial problems and mental illness, and on existing resources, training facilities, and the extent to which mental health principles are already a part of existing education programmes for health professionals. Some form of directory of mental health resources should be compiled if no similar source of data exists already.

Analysis of such data should permit a thorough assessment of the current extent of coverage of mental health by health professionals and disclose gaps in the delivery of services. It should also permit an assessment of the extent to which mental health and psychosocial skills are being used in health activities and at which levels. The needs of special groups, such as children, the mentally retarded, drug- or alcohol-dependent people, the elderly, and displaced and vagrant groups, should also be revealed.

Following this initial assessment, it is important for the planning process to establish priority targets for the development of mental health services, which should ideally be achievable within three to five years. In this, attention should be given to the components of a mental health programme outlined in Chapter 2—improvement of the functioning of general health services, contributions to overall socioeconomic development, enhancement of the quality of life, promotion of mental health, prevention of mental and neurological disorders, and treatment of mentally ill people. Initially, it may be necessary to concentrate on training needs. As an example, priorities might include:

— selection of neurological and mental disorders for management at the primary health care level;

— ensuring the provision of essential drugs required for the management of the selected priority disorders;

— establishment of a formal (and senior) administrative focal point for mental health in the ministry of health;

— strengthening of existing specialist cadres to support general health and other sector workers in the field of mental health and psychosocial development;

— training and recruitment of competent trainers;

— incorporation of a mental health component into regular teaching programmes in medical schools and other health training institutions; it is suggested that the time devoted to mental health and psychosocial skills in any health training programme should not be less than 10–15% of the total time spent in learning;

— provision of short in-service training courses in mental health for existing health staff; course curricula should include the identification and management of problems arising from drug and alcohol abuse;

— training in mental health for people working in sectors other than health.

There is considerable evidence to suggest that it is vital to have an administrative focus for mental health in the ministry of health. Without a *senior* official charged with responsibility for mental health, and the mental health component of general health care, this area tends to be neglected.

The national mental health programme should incorporate a mechanism for evaluating the adequacy of care delivered and its impact on mental health in the community, on health in general, and on the morale of patients and health staff at all levels. For evaluation to be successful there must be accurate definition of the programme's objectives, including dates for achievement of these objectives (and of all intermediate goals, where applicable).

Data acquired during the evaluation process must be fed back to planners and administrators to facilitate the continuing development and modification of the programme. Moreover, both programme development and its evaluation should be subject to regular review, on at least an annual basis, probably by the national coordinating committee and representatives from the ministry of health. The review should consider the established objectives of the programme, and assess the progress made towards achieving them. The reasons for failure should be identified, responsibility for failure allocated, and steps prescribed for setting the programme back on target. An important distinction exists between this type of review process and evaluation exercises, which seek to assess the quality of programmes.

Chapter 4

INVOLVING THE COMMUNITY

"THE PEOPLE HAVE THE RIGHT AND DUTY TO PARTICIPATE
INDIVIDUALLY AND COLLECTIVELY IN THE PLANNING AND
IMPLEMENTATION OF THEIR HEALTH CARE" (Declaration of
Alma-Ata 1978[1])

In any system of health care that seeks to provide appropriate
treatment for the sick and to promote positive health, it is essential to involve the community at every level of planning and
development. This statement is repeatedly emphasized in international declarations about health and is clearly articulated in the
Declaration of Alma-Ata. The Alma-Ata Conference also recommended "that governments encourage and ensure full community
participation through the effective propagation of relevant information, increased literacy, and the development of the necessary
institutional arrangements, through which individuals, families,
and communities can assume responsibility for their health and
well-being". Of particular importance in this is the philosophy
that communities assume responsibility in the area of health and
cease to be passive recipients of health care delivered by some
remote provider. These principles are further developed in the
Alma-Ata recommendations on primary health care, which state
". . . health reliance and social awareness are key factors in human
development. Community participation in deciding on policies
and in planning, implementing and controlling development programmes is now a widely accepted practice", and "Community
participation is the process by which individuals and families assume responsibility for their own health and welfare and for those
of the community, and develop the capacity to contribute to their
and the community's development." It is stressed further that the
community must be involved in the assessment of health situations, in the definition of problems, and in establishing priorities.

---

[1] *Alma-Ata 1978. Primary health care.* Geneva, World Health Organization, 1978, p. 3
("Health for all" Series, No. 1).

Perhaps in no area of health care are these principles more important than in that of mental health. Above all else, the principles of good mental health are concerned with people's needs, attitudes, and aspirations, and the proper satisfaction of these. Frustration resulting from the denial of basic psychological needs is a common contributing cause in individual mental breakdown and family conflict.

In providing care, and in dealing with disorders that may be incomprehensible and frightening, mental health professionals have often been alienated from the communities they serve. Ideally, good mental health care should be based on just the opposite situation:

- Its practitioners should be part of the community they serve.

- They should be perceived as understanding, sympathetic, and supportive in terms of individual, family, and community needs and problems.

- They should be seen to have a clear understanding of what the community regards as priorities.

- In the delivery of care, they should above all seek to enhance individual well-being, maintain family cohesiveness, and contribute to the socioeconomic and psychosocial development of the community.

MENTAL HEALTH WORKERS NEED TO BE CLOSE TO THOSE
THEY SERVE

In promoting these objectives, it is important that the mental health component of primary health care should be founded on knowledge of what the community identifies as problem areas. There must be constant dialogue between health workers and key groups capable of expressing fundamental community concerns and attitudes. For example, traditional healers are a rich source of information on community values, fears, ideas, and needs. They are also a valuable resource in terms of accepted methods of handling many problems at all levels. It is important that their role in community health care generally, and in mental health care in particular, be carefully defined and that they take part in the dialogue between professionals and key community groups. Other community groups with much to contribute to mental health care

are teachers, local chiefs and leaders, police officers, social and community development workers, and religious and spiritual leaders.

ASK THE COMMUNITY WHAT IT NEEDS

Through these cooperative mechanisms it should be possible for health workers to identify vulnerable families and individuals. The assessment process might be summarized as one that seeks to answer at least three fundamental questions:

- What does the community see as its mental health, psychosocial and emotional problems?

- Which members of the community are considered to be emotionally vulnerable, or at risk of psychosocial or other mental breakdown?

- What does the community believe needs to be done about such problems, either through community intervention or by the health worker or other workers?

The third question introduces the issue of the involvement of the community in improving its own mental and psychosocial health. It should be recognized that individuals, families and other groups within any community are a rich store of human wisdom and skills in communicating, in assessing need, and in providing comfort and support, but that these abilities may not always be obvious. Health workers should value the knowledge and skills of others, which may be greater than their own, and be capable of harnessing them and encouraging individuals and community groups to realize their own abilities. This is the process of promoting self-confidence within communities, leading to self-reliance in tackling a variety of mental health problems.

PEOPLE SHOULD TAKE RESPONSIBILITY FOR THEIR HEALTH

Several strategies can be employed by health workers in this process, and their study should be included in training courses. Problem-solving, self-help and common-interest groups (Alcoholics Anonymous, for example) can be highly effective in dealing with mental health issues.

People's needs, as they themselves perceive them, may sometimes involve quite unrealistic and extravagant expectations of government action, far beyond the capacity of available resources. For this reason it is important to help communities develop their own responses to mental health needs, using existing resources and community strengths. In encouraging this form of self-help, health workers must not see themselves as striving alone to mobilize community action; partnerships should be formed between health workers, between health and other development workers, and between health workers and local voluntary and nongovernmental groups. These partnerships are a vital ingredient in dealing with mental health problems at the primary health care level.

PARTNERSHIP, NOT ISOLATION

Successful community action requires that people place a high value on sound mental health, although this is initially unlikely to feature high on any list of priorities compiled by a community. It must be the task of health workers to lead people to an understanding of the importance of good mental health in improving the quality of their lives. Mental health education at the local level must be complemented by national action; for example, work done at community level to explain the nature and extent of alcohol-related problems can be reinforced by national campaigns.

This emphasis on community involvement and self-reliance should not be allowed to imply that official health facilities will become less important, or even unnecessary. Government-supported health facilities are an essential part of the equation; a balance must be achieved between the two approaches by continuing negotiation between health professionals and the community.

Chapter 5

CONTRIBUTIONS TO MENTAL HEALTH FROM OTHER SECTORS

An important concept in primary health care is that health activities should develop horizontally to involve other sectors working within the community; this demands local coordination by a designated health worker or a district health coordinating group or council. In training health workers it is important to emphasize their responsibility to maintain contacts, formal or informal, with groups and individuals within the community. Mental health care can never be adequately provided by one person working in isolation. Intersectoral collaboration, involving governmental and nongovernmental organizations, is important in all areas of health, and many groups can make major contributions to the promotion of psychological well-being within the community.

Governmental organizations

Most government ministries and paraministerial groups are organized vertically so that each has representation at grass-roots level. This is true of developed and developing societies alike. Cooperation at all levels between these groups is often very limited, and it is for this reason that the coordinated involvement of a variety of governmental and nongovernmental sectors in the development of national mental health policies and programmes has been emphasized.

Within government agencies at community level there are always trained people able to contribute to meeting community health needs; examples include schoolteachers and police officers, who are usually present in significant numbers, and generally maintain close contact with the communities in which they work.

Schoolteachers

Teachers can have a profound influence, on children and on their families, in promoting the principles of good health. Teaching physical health principles to children has traditionally been part of the teacher's role, but this has not usually extended to mental health in the past. It is important that trainee teachers be fully informed of the relevance of psychosocial factors in child development and emotional factors in learning. They should also be able to detect and cope with behavioural and emotional problems in the children they teach, and should be made specifically aware of their own role in health promotion and disease detection.

Police

In many developing countries the police also act as social workers, particularly for people with mental illness, disturbed families, abusers of alcohol and drugs, and victims of crime. Experience suggests that, if police officers are taught about mental health, and use what they learn in their dealings with the community, they can help identify some of those at risk, and can also play an important part in the detection and management of mental disorders, particularly those that excite public concern. The police are frequently called upon to control violent or potentially violent situations, which may be either domestic or of wider social significance. By applying sound mental health principles, the police should be able to contain and control these situations and avoid much needless social suffering.

Other sectors

Workers in sectors other than health—including social work, community welfare and development, agricultural extension, and any employment that involves regular and close contact with the community—may also have important roles to play in health care. Community administrators and village leaders, whether or not they have official status, can exercise considerable influence in this area.

Nongovernmental organizations

The term nongovernmental organization (NGO) is used to refer to a range of organizations, official and unofficial, which are directly or indirectly involved in a variety of social and community activities, often including health. It is therefore valuable to identify those NGOs that could contribute to health care at all levels and to consider their possible roles in supporting the introduction of a mental health component into primary health care.

NGOs as a whole, and their staff as individuals, are generally deeply committed, dynamic, and flexible, with the capacity to act quickly and the will to be innovative. They are usually well accepted by communities, to which they have ready access, and show a sensitive awareness of people's needs. It is just these qualities that make NGOs ideal to play a leading part in running a mental health care programme, capable of a pioneering role and of demonstrating what can be done.

Unfortunately, these same resources and strengths are frequently under-utilized in delivering health care, and mental health care in particular. Furthermore, there are often difficulties in developing partnerships and common endeavours between different NGOs and between NGOs and governments, and yet such collaborative undertakings would lead to better use of resources. Of the hundreds of regional, national and international NGOs, with their enormous diversity of size, scope, orientation, membership and financial resources, only about 160 are in official relations with WHO, and fewer than 20 of these are specifically concerned with mental health. Many have very limited budgets, have objectives that do not always amount to a clear policy, rarely have a full understanding of the work of other NGOs, and are often reluctant to embark on joint ventures for fear of losing their freedom of action.

Despite these and other problems of communication and funding, it is important to harness the potential of NGOs, bringing their influence to bear on the introduction of a mental health component into primary health care. In doing this, it will be essential to form new partnerships. NGO workers might be brought together at community level to discuss possible cooperation, coordination and collaboration as a means of improving their effectiveness in the area of mental health; local health workers should be encouraged to take a lead in this.

At national level, one of the NGOs (for instance a mental health association) or the government should also take the lead in creating national mental health coordinating groups. Groups of this sort should liaise with international organizations and agencies such as the United Nations Children's Fund (UNICEF), the United Nations Development Programme (UNDP), the United Nations Educational, Scientific and Cultural Organization (UNESCO), and the International Labour Office (ILO) in finding ways of promoting mental health.

COORDINATION IS ESSENTIAL

The establishment of national mental health coordinating groups is particularly important because the efficient delivery of mental health care will not only involve all health personnel at all levels of the health service, but will also require considerable intersectoral collaboration. As well as their roles in policy-making, which have already been discussed, coordinating groups should act as standing bodies in the continuing process of developing, monitoring and modifying mental health programmes. Their membership should reflect the need for input from all levels of the health system, from ministries of health down to grass roots, from other concerned public sectors and from NGOs. All these key areas should be represented, as should senior policy-makers and others with the authority to develop and implement national policy, if mental health is to be given the priority it deserves.

In shifting the emphasis from mental health care delivered in centralized facilities to its integration with primary health care, some profound changes in attitude will be essential in many sectors. It is important for key personnel in the process jointly to consider the problems of achieving this and to arrive at joint solutions.

A CHANGE IN ATTITUDE IS ESSENTIAL

In the course of developing and elaborating mental health policies, national coordinating committees should hold meetings, organize data-gathering assignments and hold discussions with community representatives. Before proceeding to more precise statements of policies and descriptions of programmes, it would then be valuable to convene a highly publicized national workshop. The need for coordination at the primary health care level should be a constant concern, and consideration should be given to developing local mental health action groups, either as independent entities or as components of local health councils. Membership of these groups should again be as wide as possible, to include representatives of NGOs, traditional healers, and the people themselves, and links between the groups and national committees should be established and maintained.

Chapter 6

INFRASTRUCTURE FOR DECENTRALIZED AND INTEGRATED MENTAL HEALTH CARE

Important principles

Before considering the infrastructure needed to support decentralized mental health care services, it is useful to summarize some of the principles that should guide the development of such services.

An awareness of the importance of sound mental health should permeate all aspects of health care, and all health-promoting activities should take full account of people's mental and emotional well-being. Health workers should be concerned not simply to treat mental disturbance but to cooperate with others in improving the psychological, as well as physical, well-being of communities.

It is essential that activities designed to promote mental health and to prevent and manage mental disorder be decentralized, with patients being cared for within, or as close as possible to, their own communities. Care of this sort should draw on community resources whenever possible.

Decentralized mental health care should be an integral part of a comprehensive health system and, where relevant, should also involve sectors other than health. Activities at secondary and tertiary levels of care should support primary-level activities, with senior mental health personnel assuming supervisory roles. To achieve this, supervisory staff will need access to adequate resources, such as training manuals, mental health education materials, and reliable supplies of essential drugs.

Mental health activities at the primary health care level should be within the competence of general health workers. Where this is the case, it will be possible to avoid isolating and thus stigmatizing patients with mental and behavioural—as opposed to physical—disorders, and to preserve a degree of confidentiality.

The type of mental health problem that can be adequately and confidently undertaken by primary health care workers is a matter for local discussion and decision. Health workers should be trained in appropriate management techniques, and the circumstances in which a supervisor must be consulted or a patient referred to a higher level of care must be clarified.

Mental health care activities should be part of health workers' everyday tasks and part of the everyday work of general health care facilities. The entire object of decentralizing this form of care will be defeated if there is any move to establish separate mental health care clinics at community level.

In applying these principles, patterns of health care delivery appropriate to the requirements and administrative structures of different countries will emerge; certain broad similarities, however, exist in many parts of the world.

The primary level

Individual communities constitute the primary level at which health care operates. Local people selected as village or community health workers are unlikely to be educated beyond primary school level or to have had more than a few months' training in basic health care principles. They may work only part-time, having a number of other family or community commitments. It would be unrealistic to expect such people to have a much more sophisticated approach to health problems than one of "common sense", although they do have the particular advantage of intimate knowledge of the community.

The sort of mental health activities that could be confidently entrusted to village health workers include monitoring the psychological—as well as physical—development of children, identifying patients suffering from major mental and neurological disorders and referring them to the next level of care, understanding the principles of long-term treatment regimes and ensuring that patients receive and take their medication, identifying cases of drug or alcohol abuse and giving appropriate advice, identifying cases of parental neglect or child abuse and taking suitable action, and undertaking limited education in mental health issues. Their cooperation with, and supervision by, better qualified primary health care workers are essential if they are to make the fullest contribution to community health care.

Primary health care workers who are sufficiently well qualified to be given supervisory responsibilities are likely to have had secondary education and two or more years' professional health training, perhaps as a nurse, medical assistant, or even general practitioner. The clinics or dispensaries from which they work may have one or two overnight beds but are principally concerned with the care of ambulatory patients.

Health workers in this category may assist, educate and supervise several village or community health workers. Additionally, they will have regular contact with visiting staff from secondary-level facilities, and should be capable of informed discussion with them about individual patients and about the mental health needs of the community as a whole.

The mental health care tasks of these clinic-based health workers include the following:

- Provision of a basic health service to both patients with mental disorders and those with physical complaints.

- Identification of mental disorders designated as priority conditions, such as epilepsy, chronic psychotic states, dependence on drugs or alcohol, and emotional and psychological crises.

- Identification of patients who should be seen by visiting secondary-level personnel or referred to a higher-level health facility.

- Identification of patients in whom physical symptoms indicate an underlying psychological problem.

- Provision of education on the maintenance of good mental health, and liaison in this with other concerned and influential members of the community.

- Keeping a register of patients referred back to the community from higher-level health facilities and maintained on long-term medication, and ensuring continuity of treatment.

- Initiation of simple programmes for personal development, such as training in relaxation techniques, promotion of recreational activities and exercise, counselling on involvement in community activities.

- Use of communication skills to mobilize and motivate mutual-support and self-help groups and to involve voluntary agencies in community development activities.

- Identification of individuals whose mental health may be under threat for any of a number of reasons, such as family stress, poverty, physical hardship, adverse working conditions, etc.

The secondary level

The secondary level of health care is generally represented by district hospitals or by large health centres serving between 50 000 and 500 000 people, although in some systems smaller health centres occupy an intermediate position between these and community clinics. Depending on their size, district hospitals will have at least one general clinician and probably a number of specialists, and should have a qualified psychiatrist, psychiatric assistant or senior nurse with specialized psychiatric training.

In existing health systems, there may be no formal administrative or functional link between district—or first-referral level—hospitals and primary health care facilities. It is important to promote close cooperation between the two, for instance by requiring district hospital staff to spend a substantial proportion of their working time visiting primary health clinics and dispensaries.

The principal functions of the specialized mental health worker at this level include the following:

- Diagnosis, treatment and follow-up of patients, including those referred from primary-level clinics. Both in- and outpatients will be seen, and the health worker should also act in a consultative capacity to other hospital departments whose patients may be suffering from disorders that are essentially psychological, rather than physical, in origin.

- Continued education, support and supervision of primary health care workers, and of personnel from other sectors concerned with mental health. To fulfil this role adequately, health workers will require training in social and behavioural sciences, community planning, and the organization and evaluation of services; where appropriate training courses do not already exist, they should be developed as a matter of urgency.

- Liaison with other relevant sectors in the district, to promote mental health, raise awareness of mental health issues both within and outside the hospital, and foster mental skills in all hospital departments.

- Application of various treatments for mental disorder, including drugs, electroconvulsive therapy and psychotherapeutic counselling.

- Efficient and comprehensive record-keeping, particularly for the follow-up and continued treatment of long-term patients who return to their communities to be cared for by primary health care workers.

The tertiary level

In mental health care, the tertiary, or second-referral, level is represented by qualified psychiatric personnel working in specialized mental health facilities, which may be independent or may be part of large general hospitals. Such specialized facilities may also be teaching institutions. At this level, mental health specialists will deal with complex problems of diagnosis and treatment referred from secondary and primary levels, organize training in mental health for all levels of the health service, have supervisory responsibilities for secondary-level facilities, undertake research and evaluation work for the entire health system, and act in an advisory capacity for governments and health administrators.

In integrating mental health care into primary health care, it is important to clarify the role of the psychiatric specialist working at the tertiary—and sometimes secondary—level. Where ignorance of mental health problems, particularly acute and psychotic disorders, is common at the primary level, specialist facilities may be inundated by referred (or self-referred) patients thought to need the type of care that can only be provided at this level. Paradoxically, many of these patients suffer from disorders that could be diagnosed and adequately managed within their own communities, and therefore represent a significant and unnecessary drain on resources.

Although it is becoming increasingly evident that nonspecialist health workers are capable of diagnosing and treating a range of mental and neurological disorders, qualified psychiatric specialists are sometimes reluctant to risk what they perceive as a loss in their own status by delegating the treatment of mental illness to general health personnel. They must come to realize that their role is increasingly one of education, consultation, supervision, research and evaluation, while their importance in the diagnosis and management of the more complex and intractable mental health problems remains undiminished. This change in emphasis demands new skills from mental health specialists, and this must be reflected in their training; further discussion of this subject may be found in Chapter 7.

The administrative—and conceptual—changes involved in this new approach to mental health care may have to be the subject of government intervention. Formal mechanisms may have to be established to control referral patterns and to modify the role played by senior mental health professionals. Above all, there must be cooperation between the various levels of health care, and sufficient flexibility in the system to ensure that health care is delivered effectively and with appropriate regard for people's differing cultural and political values.

Chapter 7

ISSUES IN TRAINING AND THE NEED FOR CHANGE

The changes proposed in methods of delivering mental health care will necessitate changes in long-established training practices for health personnel. It is not intended in this chapter to detail the training requirements for each level of health care personnel, but rather to focus on certain training principles applicable to integrated and decentralized systems of mental health care and to highlight areas that will require special attention. In doing this, it is useful to consider two pivotal areas of mental health skills.

Disease-related skills

Hitherto, only mental health specialists have acquired the skills to diagnose, assess and manage mental illness and psychological disorder. The concept of integrating mental health care with primary health care now requires that *all* general health personnel be equipped with these skills. Over the past 20 years, much has been done to define the mental health skills required by general health workers, to determine how much they are capable of learning and doing, and to produce appropriate training manuals. As a result, it has become evident that general health workers, qualified general nurses and nonspecialist doctors are able to detect and manage effectively many of the common mental and neurological diseases, with minimal reference to specialized facilities. In fact, the easiest conditions to detect—and, in many cases, to manage—are those manifested by the greatest behavioural disturbances, such as the psychoses, epilepsy, and acute states of severe emotional disorder; referral to specialized facilities is, in most cases unnecessary. However, it must be stressed that satisfactory mental health care by nonspecialized personnel relies heavily on adequate supervision from specialist staff working at secondary and tertiary levels of the health system.

Psychosocial skills

The development of psychosocial skills and sensitivity to patients' emotional and psychological problems has been mentioned frequently in this book. Patients presenting with physical symptoms may be unaware of underlying psychological causes, or may be trying "silently" to communicate deeper emotional problems. Diagnosis of the true nature of such complaints and identification of appropriate treatment or management are difficult, and health workers must learn to interview skilfully and listen carefully, setting the information gleaned in the context of patients' circumstances. Empathy with patients is essential, as is a holistic approach and an appreciation of the interdependence of psychological, emotional and physical well-being.

The need for special training in this area has often been overlooked in the past, psychosocial skills having been regarded as somehow inherent in all health workers. However, the lack of such skills, and of sensitivity and understanding, is more often a cause of dissatisfaction and complaint among patients than is lack of technical expertise, and has tended to be more marked among the more senior ranks of health professionals.

Acquisition of this type of skill and sensitivity is probably a more time-consuming and subtle process than that of learning how to treat mental illness, and relies heavily on the development of appropriate attitudes. These attitudes must be instilled early and reinforced throughout training. It is as important to allow trainees to learn from example, by observing the behaviour of senior personnel, as it is to present them with factual information.

Training principles

The content of training programmes for various levels of staff in a health care system should be determined locally, but certain important universal principles should be stressed.

Emphasis should be placed on the development of interpersonal skills, including simple counselling techniques, the teaching of relaxation and meditation techniques, empathic listening skills, and the capacity for guidance and persuasion. Local community beliefs, values and cultural attitudes should be taken into account in this area.

Where appropriate, training should be given in simple methods of diagnosis, assessment, management and referral. Flow-charts may be useful teaching aids in this context; many are available that have been developed for the more serious mental disorders and that would require only minor modification to give them local relevance. (Any teaching aids that are developed should be designed as far as possible for self-instruction, requiring minimal input from teachers.)

As far as is practicable, trainees should undertake their training in the areas where they are to practise: training in large city hospitals has little relevance to work in small rural communities. Moreover, it is essential for trainers to be familiar with the settings in which their trainees will work and to have extensive knowledge of the principles of community medicine and mental health.

Training in practical skills should be given higher priority than the teaching of theory, and should be related to locally identified mental health needs. Trends that have evolved in developed countries are not necessarily applicable to developing countries.

The training of health workers should be somewhat akin to an apprenticeship, allowing not only the teaching of skills but also the forming of desirable attitudes. This implies the need to select teachers not simply for their medical and local knowledge but for more personal traits and attributes and for practical teaching abilities as well.

Supervisory and consultative skills, which have not generally been part of training programmes, require careful consideration, with emphasis on training in the field rather than in hospitals, on the acquisition of teaching skills, and on effective supervision at a distance.

Training manuals

Many training manuals exist that are particularly valuable in developing countries, although variable in their scope.[1] The following questions will help in assessing the usefulness of any particular manual:

- Are health-related problems clearly defined within the training material?

- Are mechanisms suggested for defining such problems in the area under discussion?

- Are case examples given to illustrate these problems?

- Are suggestions made as to how students should gather their own case examples?

[1] See: *Annotated directory of mental health training manuals.* Unpublished WHO document, WHO/MNH/NAT/87.8 Rev. 1. Available from Division of Mental Health, World Health Organization, 1211 Geneva 27, Switzerland.

- Are possible solutions given to the problems posed in the case examples?

- Are students encouraged to develop their own solutions?

- Is resource material provided or catalogued which would enable students to develop solutions to the problems defined?

- Is it clear what the students will be able to do after learning, that they could not do before?

- Is any mechanism provided within the material to help students to monitor whether they have acquired the new skill?

- Are there suggestions as to how the material can be evaluated, in terms of whether a sufficient number of students have in fact learned to do something?

- Does the material encourage students to examine problems within a community and formulate solutions that require working with that community?

- Does the material encourage a multidisciplinary approach to problem-solving?

- Does the material need a teacher to get it across or could students learn from it as well or better if no teacher were available?

Chapter 8

PRIORITY CONDITIONS AND THE SUPPLY OF ESSENTIAL DRUGS

It has been established that health workers at the primary level are capable of diagnosing and managing (or referring) a wide range of mental and neurological disorders. Of these disorders it is important to define the priority conditions that should be handled at the primary level whenever possible, and this has already been done in certain countries. The list of priority conditions is likely to include psychiatric emergencies and acute psychoses, chronic psychoses, attempted suicide, certain problems relating to drug and alcohol abuse, and grand mal epilepsy; local conditions may require that this list be modified or added to.

Management of a priority condition may sometimes necessitate referral to a higher-level health facility. However, some initial emergency treatment may, even then, be given by the primary health worker, who will become involved again when the patient returns home.

Not all mental disorders require drugs in their treatment, but health workers must nevertheless have appropriate drugs at their disposal. More than 80 countries worldwide have now adopted a national list of essential drugs based on the recommendations of a WHO Expert Committee.[1] The main advantages in specifying a limited number of essential drugs are:

— fewer drugs need be purchased, stored and distributed, which means more effective management and quality control, and a lesser risk of drug abuse;

— greater possibilities for bulk purchase, resulting in lower costs;

— simplification of training for health workers.

In many parts of the world, medically unqualified personnel are constrained by law from using drugs. However, there is now extensive evidence that, with adequate supervision, relatively unskilled health workers can use many of the essential drugs safely

[1] WHO Technical Report Series, No. 770, 1988 (*The use of essential drugs*: report of the WHO Expert Committee).

and effectively, thereby avoiding unnecessary hospitalization of patients.

The essential drugs required at each level of care can be selected from the model drug list published by WHO. For the management of mental and neurological disorders the following drugs are recommended:

- *Antiepileptics*: carbamazepine, diazepam,[1] ethosuximide, phenobarbital, phenytoin, valproic acid.

- *Psychotherapeutic drugs*: amitriptyline, chlorpromazine, diazepam, fluphenazine, haloperidol, lithium carbonate.

- *Antiparkinson drugs*: biperiden, carbidopa, levodopa.

Although specific drugs are mentioned, it is the intention that most could be replaced by another from the same class, according to national policy. Correctly used, these drugs will be adequate for the management of 80–90% of mental health problems that are amenable to drug treatment. The number and type of drugs available to health workers at each level of the health service must be strictly defined according to the functions of those workers and the priority conditions they are required to handle; the more qualified the workers the more drugs they are likely to be permitted to use.

Criteria for the selection of essential drugs are set out in the report of the Expert Committee on the Use of Essential Drugs.[2]

While the appropriate drugs will have specific therapeutic effects, and will improve the morale of patients and their families by rapidly and effectively controlling aberrant behaviour, over-reliance on drugs alone is to be discouraged. A great deal can be achieved at this stage by the counselling, support and understanding that can be offered by health workers.

Certain priority conditions, and other conditions that may predispose to mental and psychological problems, can be controlled or contained without the use of essential drugs. A few examples will serve to illustrate this.

---

[1] The use of diazepam in epilepsy should be restricted to its injectable form, given intravenously or rectally for status epilepticus.
[2] WHO Technical Report Series, No. 770, 1988.

In many countries, it has been decided that the best approach to the problems of alcohol abuse is one of education. This may be provided in schools, in clinics, or in other appropriate settings by health educators, health workers, police, religious groups or other organizations or individuals with influence in the community.

The prevalence of childhood presbyopia is as high as 10% in some communities. The resulting near-blindness is a severe handicap to the education—and hence mental health—of children suffering from this complaint. Although the condition may partially resolve itself in time, the correction that can be effected with simple spectacles is immediate, and one of the most cost-effective interventions available in the field of mental health.

Where iodine deficiency is common, there is an attendant danger of children being born with irreversible brain damage caused during the first trimester of pregnancy. There is evidence that even a mild deficiency can affect mental functioning and that this is particularly apparent when children reach adolescence. It is well within the abilities of community health workers to monitor this problem and to supply iodine supplements to all women of childbearing age.

NOT ALL PRIORITY CONDITIONS REQUIRE ESSENTIAL DRUGS

The need, in certain mental and neurological disorders, for long-term *continuous* maintenance treatment makes it imperative for the supply and distribution of drugs to be properly regulated. Interruption of treatment through unavailability of essential drugs can lead to serious complications in a number of conditions. In many developing countries, public health facilities receive their drugs from a state agency, which purchases from the local manufacturers or imports from abroad. Unfortunately, these agencies are not always reliable, and clinics may find themselves without supplies of even the most basic medication. In certain circumstances, drugs may be purchased under generic names from nonprofit organizations such as ECHO (Equipment for Charitable Hospitals Overseas) and UNIPAC (UNICEF Procurement and Assembly Centre), which buy drugs of good quality and supply them at prices that compare very favourably with those of brand-name products.

Some countries, for instance Kenya and the United Republic of Tanzania, have undertaken to supply rural health facilities directly with a range of essential drugs in prepacked sealed boxes, known as ration kits. Each kit contains sufficient drugs, including phenobarbital and chlorpromazine, to satisfy the average clinic's requirements for one month. This has proved to be an efficient and cost-effective system, which has minimized losses caused by pilfering during transport.

Where no such government supply system operates, the affordability of drugs from private outlets or nongovernmental organizations must be assessed. Since the cost is likely to be high, it is most important to find some means of reconciling prescribing practices with availability of drugs, and of the cost of drugs from private sources with the needs of the community.

Chapter 9

DATA COLLECTION

If mental health care is to be decentralized and introduced as a component of primary health care, the reasons for doing this must be clear and methods of data collection must be established that will demonstrate the effectiveness, acceptability and efficiency of the new approach. There are four main purposes for which data are required:

— for planning the new type of mental health care service;

— for individual patient management;

— for day-to-day monitoring of the needs of both patients and health care facilities;

— for evaluating the impact and efficacy of the new service.

Before each of these areas is discussed in detail, some general statements must be made about the whole process of data collection, transfer and management.

General principles

Only data that are genuinely relevant, and essential to the performance of a specific task, should be routinely collected. For example, primary health care workers require information on which of their patients need regular medication, on the precise frequency and dosage of medication, on the action to take if patients do not comply with treatment regimens, and on when individual cases need to be reviewed. The exact nature of the data will vary according to the type of health facility and the community served, but information will generally be entered in some kind of clinical register. Provided that health workers are aware of the need for efficient follow-up of each patient, this type of data collection should present no problems.

Supervisory personnel also require access to this type of data in order to advise and support primary health workers and to evaluate their work. Additionally they will need to be aware of total numbers of patients seen, diagnoses made, and referrals to higher-level health facilities. Feedback from supervisors on the basis of their assessment of these data will help primary health care workers to appreciate their role in the overall mental health care programme and reinforce their awareness of the need for accurate and relevant data.

Further reinforcement comes from personal contact in the transfer of data. Informal discussions between primary health care workers and their supervisors, during visits by the latter to health care facilities, afford excellent opportunities for the direct exchange of information, for clarification of the purposes of good record-keeping, for identification and solution of problems, and for training.

> PERSONAL CONTACT IS IMPORTANT IN THE
> EXCHANGE OF INFORMATION

To maintain the accuracy and relevance of data, methods of data collection should be regularly reviewed. Where it becomes obvious that certain types of data are not being used, their collection should be abandoned. Discussion with health workers at all levels is valuable in reaching this type of decision; the data collected are likely to be more accurate if those collecting them are convinced of their significance.

Routine collection of data on total populations, against the day when some specific research question may need to be addressed, is of doubtful value. Again, the problem is often one of inaccuracy of data through ignorance of their usefulness. Where a specific situation is to be investigated, or new intervention evaluated, far more reliable results are likely to be obtained by a specialized research team employing sampling techniques on a proportion of the target population.

Data required for planning

If a new type of health care service is to be established, data will be required by planners, by the ministry of health, and probably by national coordinating committees. Epidemiological data on mental health are likely to be derived from research in particular communities and will include information on the probable prevalence and incidence of mental health problems and on the extent to which these are dealt with by existing health care facilities. Other data may come from research carried out in pilot projects or in other countries.

Planners should be aware of and, where appropriate, use data from other countries. If clear answers to specific questions have been obtained in other similar societies, there is likely to be little advantage in repeating research. For example, various countries worldwide have reported that between 20% and 40% of all patients seen in general health clinics are suffering primarily from psychological disorders. It is unlikely that a fresh survey will produce a significantly different figure.

The value of informal data in the planning process should be stressed. The opinions and observations of experienced clinicians, administrators, academics and fieldworkers are of direct relevance to planners. Much of the impetus for decentralizing mental health care and making greater use of nonspecialist health workers has come from just such informal beginnings.

If the advice given elsewhere in this book is followed, planners will establish achievement targets for proposed new programmes; these targets should be borne in mind in identifying the data required for evaluating the results of the programmes. It is also essential that primary health care workers understand how their work contributes to the achievement of targets; the data they collect are then more likely to be willingly recorded and accurately reported.

Data for patient management

The data required by primary health care workers for the organization of their everyday tasks consist largely of the names and addresses of all patients seen, with details of the drugs they are receiving, in what dosages and with what frequency. In particular, some kind of register should be developed for patients with chronic illnesses. Efficient record-keeping of this type should ensure that no patient is lost to follow-up.

While supervisors will not need all of this information for the performance of their own jobs, it is essential that they instil an understanding of its importance into primary health workers and supervise its continued and conscientious collection. They may find it valuable to discuss with primary health workers suitable forms of clinical register for the simple and efficient recording and later retrieval of such basic data.

Data for health service management

The everyday management of the health service, and the monitoring and management of health clinics, require a considerable input of data, particularly as regards primary health care and its interface with second-level care. The principal uses of these data are in planning, evaluation and decision-making. Straightforward and relevant information on patient care, collected by primary health workers, should be given directly to supervisory staff whenever possible. The data are needed by supervisors to evaluate the staff for whom they are responsible and to provide appropriate support (for instance ordering drugs and supplies), and include the following:

— total number of patients seen

— number of different diagnoses made

— the frequency with which patients are seen

— number of patients referred to higher-level health facilities

— number of chronically ill patients seen

— the frequency with which chronically ill patients are visited at home

— number of families identified as being at risk of mental health problems

— numbers and types of drugs used to treat different disorders

— stock levels of drugs and other supplies held by clinics

— projected needs for drugs and other supplies over the next planning period

— the frequency and nature of interactions between health facilities and other sectors.

Evaluation of services

In evaluating the success of a new mental health care programme in meeting the targets identified by its planners, much information can be gleaned from the same sources of data that contribute to the programme's everyday management. The purpose of evaluation is to assess:

— effectiveness (in reaching targets and achieving maximum coverage)

— efficiency (in the use of resources)

— impact (on overall mental and physical health)

— relevance (to the needs of the population).

The extent of coverage achieved by the programme can be assessed from such information as the following:

— numbers of patients with particular disorders seen and/or treated at each level of the health care system

— number of patients treated and discharged compared with number needing long-term maintenance treatment.

Information on the treatments used in different disorders, the quantities of different drugs prescribed and the proportion of patients responding to treatment will be indicators of the efficacy of the mental health programme. The impact of the programme in a particular area may be monitored by determining the number of patients presenting with particular problems or disorders over a given period of time. This information will also be valuable to senior managers, who have to ensure an appropriate allocation of resources. Data should also be available on the frequency of visits to clinics by supervisory personnel, which will enable their performance to be evaluated, and on contacts between health personnel and other sectors, which will indicate the degree of intersectoral cooperation. All data should be strictly relevant to the assessment being made; a clear answer to the question "Why are these particular data essential?" should be possible.

Certain research questions, however, can only be addressed with data that are not available in the normal course of health work. The collection of specific research data of this nature is probably not a task that should be delegated to primary health workers.

The data collection process and subsequent discussion of the results and conclusions are also valuable in the context of training, enabling health workers to monitor the effectiveness of their activities and identify areas of deficiency.

Indicators for service assessment

Qualitative observations on the organization of a health service are as essential to the evaluation process as numerical data, and will provide valuable indications of whether or not a health programme's objectives are being achieved. Following the principles outlined in this book, such observations should provide insight into the extent to which:

— mental health services have been decentralized

— mental health services have been integrated with general health services

— mental health care is being delivered at the primary health care level

— other organizations, governmental and nongovernmental, are involved in mental health care

— mental health care is being made available to disadvantaged sections of the population, such as refugees, urban migrants, and neglected children.

Evaluation of progress in these areas requires certain measurable indicators to be established, and consequently certain types of data to be available. Assessment of the extent of mental health care delivery outside specialized mental hospitals, e.g.

— in general hospitals

— in peripheral health centres, both rural and urban

— as services in areas other than traditional psychiatric disciplines, such as drug dependence, mental health of children, and psychogeriatrics,

will reveal the degree of penetration of mental health concerns into all areas of the health system and to all sections of the population.

The extent to which the national mental health programme conforms to generally accepted principles of planning and development will be revealed by answers to questions such as the following:

● Is there a national mental health policy?

● If there is, does the policy accord with the national policy on general health issues?

● Is the policy sufficiently broad to embrace areas such as drug and alcohol dependence? If not, are these aspects covered by other declared government policies?

- Has the national mental health programme clearly specified target-oriented activities and laid down dates for the achievement of objectives?

A broad mental health programme should specify the direction to be followed in carrying out stated policies. To evaluate its success in doing this, the following types of question should be asked:

- Have priority disorders been defined for initial treatment at primary health care level? If so, what are they?

- Has a list of essential drugs for the management of these priority disorders been drawn up?

- Are mechanisms in place for maintaining the supply of essential drugs?

- Are measures specified for the control of all psychoactive drugs with potenital for abuse?

- Have steps been taken to initiate training in mental health for all general health workers, particularly those at the primary health care level?

- Have reorientation and training workshops been developed for senior health personnel, to develop their knowledge and skills in the area of mental health?

- Is there a logical structure within the health system for the referral of patients to higher- or lower-level health facilities and for the supervision by specialist staff of less qualified personnel?

- Are there directives for community involvement in the delivery of mental health care?

- Have mechanisms been established for the involvement of other sectors in the mental health programme?

- What is the nature of participation by nongovernmental organizations in the mental health programme?

- Has suitable provision been made for the regular collection, transfer and analysis of appropriate data, and for the feedback of results and conclusions to the personnel concerned?

These questions are presented only as typical examples and may well need modification to suit the characteristics of individual national mental health programmes. The answers will be valuable to ministries of health and other government bodies concerned with national mental health policy in assessing the extent and rate of its implementation and for purposes of comparison with data from other countries.

Other types of evaluation, such as assessing whether or not the cost of a mental health care programme is offset by savings in other areas, whether readmission rates for patients with particular disorders have been reduced, or the extent to which various mental disorders are being detected in particular parts of the country, may best be performed through formal research projects. Such projects can sometimes be valuably incorporated into training courses; health personnel at all levels can benefit greatly from undertaking small research projects and possibly presenting the results in the form of dissertations. Long-term projects, covering several aspects of the mental health care programme, can be carried out by consecutive groups of trainees. The more that health workers can be encouraged to take an interest in this type of activity and to extend it to their work, constantly monitoring the mental health needs of communities and the responses of the health service, the greater will be their appreciation of the importance of mental health care in its widest sense.

Chapter 10

THE COST OF A MENTAL HEALTH COMPONENT IN PRIMARY HEALTH CARE

The aim of the proposals outlined in this book is to concentrate attention on mental health problems and to improve the delivery of mental health care. At first sight, the proposals might seem to imply extensive financial outlay, but there is good evidence to suggest that this need not be the case. Mental health problems—especially as an underlying cause of, or resulting from, physical complaints—are frequently a considerable drain on health resources as a consequence of being misunderstood or misdiagnosed. There is every reason to suppose that introducing an effective mental health programme into primary health care will alleviate this situation and that, with proper budgetary planning and allocation of resources, it can actually reduce overall health costs.

In countries that already have a primary health care system, or are developing one, health workers should be able to incorporate mental health promotion, plus prevention and treatment of mental illness, into their everyday work. Where a mental health component has already been successfully integrated into primary health care, the cost has proved to be very low, especially in small countries that are fairly densely populated. Increasing the attention given to mental health by health personnel—and by workers in other concerned sectors—need not be expensive in either time or money, and will enhance the efficacy of the health care system as a whole. Mental health care, unlike many other areas of health, does not generally demand costly technology; rather, it requires the sensitive deployment of personnel who have been properly trained in mental health and psychosocial skills.

Despite the long-term benefits and financial savings, however, there are several areas in which expense will be incurred. First there is the cost of training activities for health personnel; curricula will require revision, and workshops, teaching materials, manuals and practical guides will be needed. Second, there is the expense of appointing key personnel, with responsibility for mental health, in ministries of health at national and possibly regional level. Allied to this will be the costs of establishing and running national mental health coordinating groups and local mental health action committees. In many cases, however, people working in this capacity will do so on a voluntary basis or will undertake their duties as an extension of existing governmental responsibilities.

Staffing costs at the primary level should be minimal if mental health activities are undertaken by existing general health personnel; adding the subject of alcohol abuse, for example, to an established health education programme should not involve significant expense. It should be appreciated, however, that the adequacy of a programme implemented at primary health care level will depend to a great extent on the strength of support provided at secondary and tertiary levels, and it is here that expansion may be needed in some countries. It is important to establish clear estimates of staff numbers necessary to maintain the more specialized levels of care, and then assess whether national resources are adequate for the recruitment, training and continuing employment of such people.

The cost of providing essential drugs may well be relatively high, particularly if the national policy is to supply them free of charge. The need to maintain uninterrupted supplies must also be considered in this context. Expense may also be incurred for appropriate and reliable transport, without which a primary health care service cannot function effectively. Senior staff must be able to maintain close contact with those whom they supervise, which may often entail travelling to outlying clinics.

Where a pilot scheme is planned as an initial step in implementing a mental health programme, costs must be carefully assessed. Because of the pioneering nature of such schemes, and the fact that they frequently involve research, they may prove relatively expensive. Where the intention is ultimately to introduce the same scheme on a countrywide basis, the costs of doing this must be assessed at the time the pilot scheme is planned; even without the research element, an over-elaborate scheme translated to a national scale may prove to be too costly to support.

Consideration could valuably be given to the extent to which services provided by NGOs, private hospitals and industrial health schemes can contribute to the national programme. Where nongovernmental hospitals and health facilities exist, it may well be that a proportion of the population prefer to spend their own money on health care, and this can be an important factor in assessing the costs of a mental health programme. Careful deliberation is essential, however, if such a diverse pattern of health care delivery within a single country is to be harmonized with other economic and ideological considerations.

Finally, when estimating the overall costs of introducing a mental health component into primary health care, it is important to take full account of the savings that could be effected by the scheme. In countries where a mental health programme has been successfully implemented, two main areas of potential savings have been identified.

Many existing programmes of care for the mentally ill are exceedingly wasteful of the skills and time of specialist personnel, particularly where large numbers of patients are referred to centralized tertiary facilities and subsequently hospitalized. The specialists involved in treating these patients could be more economically and more effectively deployed in other parts of the health service, spending a greater part of their time in an educational and supervisory capacity. Many of their patients could be just as effectively—often more effectively—managed by less specialized personnel at the community level, provided that adequate and continuing support, in the form of essential drugs and appropriately trained primary health workers, were available. Where this type of support can be made available, repeated relapse and readmission of patients to specialist facilities can be minimized.

The costs incurred by failure to diagnose certain mental disorders represent a second area in which savings are possible. Studies in various countries have revealed that, at the point of first referral to medical facilities, at least 20% of patients presenting with physical complaints are in fact suffering from mental or psychological disorders. Where the underlying problem is misdiagnosed, or not diagnosed at all, expensive medication may be prescribed unnecessarily, and repeated, often complex, clinical investigations may be undertaken. Moreover, patients are likely to attend clinics repeatedly in the sincere belief that they are suffering from serious physical disorders. This represents an alarming wastage in the work done by health personnel, in the drugs prescribed, and in the use of valuable resources. The situation can be largely avoided if health personnel at all levels receive suitable training in mental health skills, which will allow them to recognize, and treat appropriately, those patients in whom physical symptoms are a manifestation of an underlying psychological disorder.